I dedica...

My daughter, Kalli and my son, Ray

*I love you with all my heart. May this book be a reminder of all God has done in our lives. My prayer is that you will let God take away the hurt and confusion of the past as I have and move on to a happy, peaceful life. I pray blessings and protection over your lives every day. God still cares about you now just like
He did then and so do I.*

Always remember- I love you!

ALSO

My mom and her husband, Patsy and Herman Williams, my sister, Ruth Suire, my brother, James Franklin and the rest of my family

May this book reveal to you the details of my life so that you may understand why I am what I am and why I made the decisions I did. You were always so understanding when you knew something was wrong, yet you never pressured me to tell why. I'm so blessed to have a close and loving family. Thank you for all your support. I love you all very much!

Acknowledgements

I would like to thank my pastor and his wife, Bro and Sis James H. Whitehead for being there for me during this distressing time in my life. They prayed with me, cried with me and were a real comfort to me. They helped me in so many ways. I will always love them and I appreciate them for everything they did for me.

I would also like to thank all my friends at Leesville First United Pentecostal Church, Leesville, LA and my friends at Fountain of Life Pentecostal Church, Natchitoches, LA for all their prayers and support over the last 27 years.

I would especially like to thank my special friends Debbie Carter, Tonya Pagels, and Rita Carpenter who has cried with me, prayed for me, sent me cards of encouragement, etc. For all your phone calls, all the times you let me cry on your shoulder, for all the times you just come and sit with me and listened not knowing what to say- I thank you and love you very much.

I thank my husband, Don, for standing beside me through good and bad, for being strong in the face of defeat when I felt like giving up, for holding me through tears and nightmares that woke him up in the middle of the night and for just loving me like I am. You are the love of my life, my best friend and hunting buddy. Thank you for loving me.

Most of all, I want to thank my God, whose name is Jesus. For without Him I would not be here today to tell my story. My story would have been a lot different without His mercy and His grace on my life. Thank you with all my heart. Your love is so amazing!

Is This Really My Life???

Forward

It has been an honor to have Kim Collins call me Pastor for over fifteen years. During this time, she has been an unwavering child of God. I knew of some of her trauma, but was not aware of the severity of it. This book is written from a desire to help others, and is a must-read for anyone in an abusive relationship or trying to help someone in a traumatic situation. There is no fiction here, but only the transparency of a heart that knows what it is to hurt and wants to tell others that there is hope and that they can survive with God's help.

JAMES H. WHITEHEAD

Is This Really My Life???

INTRODUCTION

I was born in Shreveport, LA and moved to Leesville when I was 2 years old. I grew up in the country and went to a little Baptist country church called Oak Forest Baptist Church. We were faithful to attend every service. My mom did not let us miss for anything except for being sick enough to run a fever. We even went to church when we were on vacation. I loved Sunday School and hearing about Jesus. My sister, Ruth and I used to play church when we were little. We used to baptize each other in the bathtub then we would preach and sing to each other. I started memorizing scripture when I was very young and won a lot of Sunday night Bible drills.

I mostly loved to read and hear about missionaries, especially ones from other countries.

We were a typical happy family. My dad worked at Fort Polk Army Base and my mom was a housewife. We always looked forward to our dad coming home in the evenings. Mom would say, "It's time for Daddy-watch for him!" Ruth and I would hop up on the couch and look out the window until he arrived home. He would always pick up both of us when he came in.

I remember singing with my sister Ruth and my dad when we were very young. We sang, "I Wouldn't Take Nothing for my Journey Now". I could see my mom smiling proudly as we sang. She always made us matching dresses to wear to church. I also remember when we acted up in church (we weren't allowed to even whisper in church) my dad would thump us on top of the head. If we still acted up, he would say, "Just wait 'til we get home". I would be so nervous about our spanking after church I couldn't pay attention any more. He didn't forget either.

I'm so thankful to have had a daddy that loved us enough to correct us and try to make good people out of us even though we did not see that at the time. He always came to us after our spanking and talked to us about why he had to punish us. He cried sometimes and we did too. I had rather take the spanking than listen to the talking. We knew he loved us. He played with us on the floor and out in the yard. He was such a good daddy.

One Saturday, we had gone with Mom to get her hair fixed and when we returned home, my dad was lying on the kitchen floor. He always played with us on the floor so Ruth and I jumped on top of him and started tickling him. When my mom came in, we could tell by the look on her face that something was wrong. She was yelling, "Get off him! Get off him!" with a tearful voice. So we backed up and watched. My dad had died of a massive heart attack. He was only 47 years old. My mom was left to raise my brother, James, 2; my sister, Ruth, 7; and myself at age 9 all by herself.

The next few years were mostly full of sadness and depression for me. I didn't want to do my school work. My mom was sick a lot and we stayed with some family friends while she would be in the hospital. I was molested during that time by the man of the house that we called Uncle John*. His sons tried it too (they were a good bit older than me), but he got on to them. Aunt Susie* would be gone somewhere and he would make all the kids play outside…except for me. (* The prior two names have been changed) I had to go to the bedroom with him. I never told anyone until last year. This was a painful and embarrassing, memory so I chose to put it out of my mind years ago. Only last year was I made to think of it because of an illness I had that caused the doctor to ask about an abusive past.

In my teen years we had all healed pretty well and moved on with the life God gave us. It was a hard road for my mom to be Dad and Mom, but she did well by us. She gave us everything we needed and a lot of what we wanted when she could. She taught us that you didn't have to spend money to have fun. You didn't have to have fancy things to be blessed. She taught us that family was first, after God of course, and never to go to bed mad at each other. She taught us that we were more blessed than some others that had more because we loved each other.

My mom was really involved in missionary work and spoke about it a lot at ladies meetings. We always went to summer church camp and went on some other church trips when we could. Our life was all about church. I loved hearing missionary stories of how God brought them thru tough times. My favorite to read about was Annie Armstrong and Lottie Moon. I also liked Corrie Ten Boom. I always thought I would grow up to be a missionary or a pastor's wife though now being close friends with my pastor's wife, I'm glad God knows best.

When I was about 15, I was suddenly ready to be an adult (or so I thought). I didn't want to be told what to do or when to do it. I didn't need to know all that stuff in school because I wasn't going to be a teacher or accountant. I wanted to be a housewife and mother and devote my life to my family like my mom did. So I started to date and go out with friends that I went to school with. We drank beer a little bit and hung out together and just did what teenagers did back then. I never tried drugs or cigarettes (thank God). I only drank beer because I wanted to fit in. I really didn't like it at all. One night we were all at my friend's house and his parents weren't home so we got into their liquor supply. They dared me to down a beer (a malt liquor beer at that) in less than a minute. Well, I wasn't going to be a party pooper, so down it went. By the time I finished it, they were all laughing. It wasn't long until that beer hit me like a ton of bricks. I got up on the pool table and laid down. I just wanted to sleep or throw up or something. I was miserable. They put me in the car so I could be home by my curfew and I left headed for home. We lived three miles out in the country so I had a long drive. I remember sitting up on the edge of the seat holding on to the steering wheel with both hands and praying for God to help me get home. I would go across the line a little and then come back and go off the shoulder a little. I was only driving about 45mph. When I got home I barely made it to the bathroom in time for it all to come up. I thought all my insides were coming out. I was on the floor in the bathroom when I heard the door barely open. My mom looked in and then shut the door. I knew I was in trouble. I went on to bed that night and Mom never said a word. She didn't have to. She knew I would never do that again. I still felt it the next day. I never even liked the smell of beer after that.

I was still 15 when I met Ray. We dated for a couple months and decided to get married. He would tell me of how he did his girlfriends before me. He told me about their fights, about him leaving them on the side of the road, and how he took one home and went to pick up another one. But, naïve little ole me knew that when you got married, all those things stopped because it's you and him together forever and no one will come between you. Right? Whatever comes up, we can handle it together. I could not wait to get married and become a grown-up. I now would have the respect that I wanted and I could make my own decisions. My mom said we had to wait until I was at least 16, so we did.

We got married the next weekend after my 16th birthday. I quit school in the tenth grade and got a GED (a decision I will always regret). We moved off to Vidor,

TX and then to Corpus Christi, TX to work. After we had been married for 2 months, I found out I was pregnant with our first child. Ray Jr was born November 6, 1979. We called him Little Ray. I was instantly in love with him from the moment I held him for the first time.

Not long after he was born, I saw the side of Ray that I had no clue about. Ray got mad at me about something and shoved me down on the bed while I was holding Little Ray. I was in total shock. I had never been around anyone with a bad temper before. How could a daddy take a chance on hurting his child and why would he want to hurt me? I was supposed to be the love of his life, his sweetheart, and the mother of his child. I had no idea what was ahead. This was the beginning of a 26 year journey of survival.

CHAPTER 1

A Tough Start

Ray was never fair with me. He said "there's no such thing as fair". He never wanted me to know how much money he made or had on him. Any time I asked him about money, he would always say "five dollars". He did not like for me to have friends, so I had to quit talking to them. He only wanted me to be friends with his mom and dad and my mom and sister. He would leave me a quarter so I could call him at work if I needed him.

My mother-in-law did not like me because I was not Pentecostal. She wanted Ray to marry a Pentecostal girl so she knew I wasn't for him. She knew I wasn't going to look like a Pentecostal and that I was definitely not going to be one. His dad didn't like me either because I was raised without a dad (like I could have changed that) and he thought I was spoiled. My mother-in-law and I had quite a few harsh words for each other over the next few years. Ray's dad died in 1981 and Ray took it very hard. His dad was his idol. He started drinking more after that.

Things got somewhat better between my mother-in-law and me. I started going to the Pentecostal church with her sometimes. She loved to show off her grand-son. When I first went to church with her, I just sat there amused at all the liveliness going on. We were taught to be reverent in church. These people all said "amen" and "halleluiah" every few minutes and clapped their hands when the preacher was preaching. When it came time to pray, EVERYBODY prayed together. It was noisy. It was nothing like my church. Usually a deacon prayed and everyone else was perfectly silent. I was kind of spooked when I heard someone talking in a language I couldn't understand. "Did they know how foolish they looked?" was my thought. I would never do that. Anyways, I didn't want to live for God right now. I was young and liked to do things that you couldn't do if you belonged to a church.

Things at home were ok most of the time as long as I did what I was told. But if Ray was having a bad day or something went wrong, he would take it out on me. One morning before I got out of bed, he was getting ready for work and couldn't find something. So he gets mad and hits me with his belt across my thigh like a whip and leaves a big whelp down the side of my leg. I decided while he was gone to move back to my mom's house and get away from him. I hurried and got my mom's friends to help and warned them that if they saw him coming to leave as soon as they could because he would hurt them. We moved everything I could (which wasn't much) before he came home. When he found out, he came to my mom's and apologized and said he loved me and wanted me to come home and it would never happen again. Again, naïve little ole me believed him and I went back home with him. He sent his employees to get our stuff. It didn't take me long to realize nothing had changed.

He liked to go out "with the guys" after work for a few drinks and shoot pool, only it turned out that he left home with guys but ended up with girls. One night after he and one of his friends went out, they came home way after midnight and I acted like I was asleep. I heard Ray telling about everything in detail of what took place that night with the girl he was with. I was hurt so bad. My heart was pounding, but I knew not to say a word or he would beat my head off. He continued to go out a couple times a week and when I would ask to go with him, he would get mad and say, "All you would do is just get me in a fight! I'll be back in a little while!" He would always make me iron a pair of jeans and a shirt for him when he went out. I could hardly stand it. My insides would be churning and I would be shaking all over thinking about him going out with someone else to have fun and I have to stay home and babysit our child.

3

I was very particular about who I left my son with and I wanted to do right by him so I bit my lip and stayed home.

Ray would never give me any money to spend so I decided to get a job at a local department store. I had him to take me to work every day and pick me up in the evenings because we only had one truck. I never knew if he would be there or not. Many nights I would stand outside on the covered sidewalk of the store and wait while it was raining and cold for him to pick me up. Everyone else had left and I was afraid because it was dark. One night I kept trying to call him from the payphone because he had not picked me up yet and I never could get him to answer. So, I got his mom to come get me and when I got home, he was on the couch with the babysitter watching TV. I quit my job before long. I felt like I was fighting a losing battle. What little money I received for working he made me spend on groceries and bills so I still didn't have any spending money.

CHAPTER 2

Sweet Revenge...
Or Was It?

I was getting tired of Ray acting like a single man while I was staying at home, being a housewife and mom. I just wanted to be loved and appreciated. Ray worked out of town a lot and he asked his policeman friend to come and check on me several times a night to make sure I didn't go anywhere. We started talking outside each night. It wasn't long before

I was looking forward to seeing him each night and one thing lead to another and you can guess the rest. After all, Ray was gone to see other girls and sometimes stayed the whole night. He once told me about an older rich lady in the town he was working in that couldn't keep her hands off him and begged him to spend the night while her husband was gone. So why shouldn't I have a little enjoyment; a little something to look forward to. I just wanted to be loved.

We started meeting away from the house and I was so nervous. I was just about a basket case the whole time I was in this relationship. I wanted to have a friend, but I knew I was doing wrong and just because Ray was doing it did not mean it was right for me to do it. Besides, I knew Ray would kill me and him too if he caught us. My nerves got so bad that I would wake up every morning covered in hives. I ended the relationship shortly because I couldn't stand the guilt and I would constantly be mad at myself because my conscious was beating me up all the time. Didn't Ray have a conscious? Why could he get by with it and I couldn't? Maybe that's why he drank so much.

My hives continued and I went to several different doctors and had all kinds of tests run and all they could tell me was that it was my nerves. They put me on Anti-depressants to help me get myself together, but all they did was make me like a zombie. I would take them mostly when I knew I could stay home because I could hardly function while I was on them. I remember someone asking me a question one day and by the time they were thru talking I couldn't remember what they just said to give them an answer. I must have looked like an idiot. I knew I had to do something. I was afraid something would happen to Little Ray and I wouldn't be at myself enough to handle it. After all, I had to be the responsible one at our house. I had to grow up quick and be the mom and the dad as much as I could.

I started back going to the Baptist church with my mom thinking that if I got involved in church I would feel better. I was so depressed and afraid all the time. I knew Ray was going to kill me any day because the angry outburst and threats were happening more often. At church, I enjoyed the young adult class, but when it came time for preaching all I could do is cry. I can't count the times I got up and left in the middle of church to go home because I couldn't stop crying. Then I would quit going to church for a while. Maybe if I didn't go I wouldn't think about it as much. I wanted to live right, but somehow I knew there should be more than what I learned about at church. Even when I was a small child I always knew there should be more. I was baptized twice when I was young just to try to help me feel more saved.

So, I started going back to the Pentecostal church with my mother-in-law for a while. I loved what I felt there. I felt God's love and wanted more, but I didn't let myself cry because I didn't want any of those people coming over and laying their hands on me and getting loud with their praying. That would be embarrassing. That looked so foolish to me. I was raised to believe that all you had to do is believe that Jesus died for my sins and I would be saved. But if that's so, the devil would be saved because he certainly believes in God. My mother-in-law would tell me, "wouldn't it be better to have too much than not enough?" The main thing that bothered me was the dress standards at her church. I loved jewel-ry. I wore a ring on every finger and some toes. I had lots of earrings and necklaces for every outfit. And I would never wear a dress around the house or out in the yard or even to work. I worked at a plant nursery. How dumb would that look to wear a dress with rubber boots? I also loved the beach. Me, go to the beach with a dress on…I don't think so! The main thing was my makeup and hair. I never let anyone see me without makeup and fingernail polish. I had a bad complexion and covered it with makeup. And my hair had to be perfect. I colored it and cut it every few months to keep it perfect. I was very particular about the way I looked. So, there was no way I was going to join this church and I quit going to it and went back to my mom's church. This went on for about 5 years back and forth. I was so miserable.

I was afraid all the time. Ray made comments like, "One of these days I'm going to be in here cleaning my gun and it's going to go off and kill you and no one will ever know the difference." I knew he was right be-cause he always got out of every kind of trouble he got in to. One night he was out fooling around and a guy backed into his new Corvette. He was already drunk, so he busted a beer bottle and used is on this guy's face. He put him in the hospital for several months even hav-ing reconstructive surgery and all Ray had to do was pay him a couple thousand dollars. No fines or jail time. They let him off.

He even tried several times to put a loaded gun in my hand when we would be fighting so he could kill me in self-defense. After all, the only story would be his. A dead person can't talk. Somehow, God gave me the strength to keep my hand closed every time so it never happened. I say that God gave me strength because Ray was very strong and stout in his arms and legs so I know it had to be God. I have never seen him beaten at arm wrestling.

CHAPTER 3

"God, Please Help Me!"

My nerves were getting worse by the day and sometimes I would ask God to just take my life. I could never kill myself, but I told God that I hated my life and wanted out. I would look up to God and say, "Is this really my life? Why did I get a husband and a life like this?" Then I would think about Little Ray to be left without me to care for him and I sure didn't want to leave him. I would go back to the Pentecostal church and feel the moving of God on me. I wanted to feel God and then I would look around at how all the ladies looked and knew I didn't want to look like that. I would go home and be afraid all week long because I didn't move when God told me to and I knew my time would run out before long. How long would God give me before He would say, "this is the last call for you"? I was scared to even go anywhere because I may have a wreck and die before I got a chance to go back to church and give my heart to God. I had no idea what a merciful and longsuffering God we have. I was about to have a nervous breakdown. Finally, I was to the place where I said, "God, show me if this is the only way for me to be saved and go to Heaven. Is this the only way to really have the peace that I am looking for? Let me see it and understand it for myself."

I never took people's word for things too much; I wanted to know it for myself. I had been reading my Bible some during the weeks before, but just couldn't get it. After asking God to show me the way, reading the Bible was like reading a new book. Everything was as plain as day. I see that you do have to have God's Spirit inside you to go to Heaven and when that happens you speak in a new language that only God knows the meaning of as described in the book of Acts. It is such a miracle. And then you are baptized in Jesus' name for the remission of your sins. I had been baptized in the titles Father, Son, and Holy Ghost before but not in Jesus' name like the Bible says. Then I got to thinking that it wouldn't be so bad to wear a dress and let my hair grow and not wear makeup anymore if I could feel peace. Those things just were not important any more. I made up my mind that I wanted the Holy Ghost for myself, but I was afraid of what I would look like so I went and got my hair cut about 2 weeks before I got the Holy Ghost. (God was merciful to even give me the Holy Ghost after doing that). I also didn't want to open myself up and pray in front of all my friends so I got a friend of mine to go with me to the Pentecostal church in Anacoco. She and I could both get it there where we didn't know anyone and then come back to my own church. Well, it didn't work like that. We prayed and she got the Holy Ghost, but I didn't. The whole time I was praying, I could hear, "Go back to your church". So I did the next Sunday.

By then my friend had already backslid so I went by myself. When I went in people started hugging me and saying, "I hear you are seeking the Holy Ghost! That's great!" I don't even remember what the preacher preached about or what songs were sung. When the alter service started, my hands were sweating and shaky, but I took off to the altar to give God a chance to help me. I was desperate. No one knew what I had been going through. I had to have God. If Ray did kill me, at least I would not go to hell. The tears started flowing and people started praying all around me and I didn't care anymore what I was looking like. I needed help and I was desperate. David and Linda Larwood were praying with me. I remember opening my eyes and seeing David right up in my face praying so hard his face was red. I had already made friends with them. I guess what impressed me most is that they were friends with me even though I didn't have the Holy Ghost. She didn't judge me or make me feel evil because I wasn't like them. Then, as the tears were flowing I started telling God (after I repented of every sin I could think of) that I wanted Him more than anything. The new language started coming out and people all around me were jumping up and down. I felt like a heavy weight was gone off me and I felt a peacefulness that I cannot explain. I was immediately baptized in Jesus' name and I have never felt more pure in my life. I knew I found what I had been looking for all my life. I knew I had God in my heart without a doubt. No one could tell me that it wasn't real because I experienced it for myself. It was only the goodness of God that led me to repent (Romans 2:4). Isn't it wonderful that God said, "Ye have not chosen me but I have chosen you"… (John 15:16) I felt it such a privilege to be chosen by God to live full of His spirit. Who was I to be so blessed? I had not done anything good to deserve being called of God. I was 21 years old when I received the Holy Ghost and it just gets better every day.

CHAPTER 4

My New Life

I was so excited and went home and told Ray. He didn't have too much to say. It hurt a little that he wasn't happy about it but that was ok because I was a changed woman and I wasn't going to let him rob me of my experience. The next day I cleaned out my closet and called my girlfriend. I told her to come get it all and that I would not be wearing that stuff anymore. I WANTED to look holy. I gave her my makeup and jewelry and my old music that I would not need any more. I threw away all my anti-depression pills and never took another one to this day. That's not to say I didn't feel like I needed one a time or two. But instead of taking a pill, I got on my knees and told God I needed Him to help me. Being in the presence of our merciful and loving God is an experience like no other and can fix any state of mind you may be in. His love and understanding would cover me and in a little while I would be just fine.

Two weeks after I received the Holy Ghost, I had to take my son to have some warts removed off his eyes. When the doctor gave him the shot above his eye, I fainted and fell back and hit my head on a chair. Later that evening when my headache kept getting worse, Ray took me to the emergency room thinking maybe I had a concussion or something. They took me in and x-rayed my head at several angles. They kept coming in and out and taking more x-rays. Then they left out and were gone for a long time. When they finally came back, they said that the hit on my head caused my head-ache but there was no damage from that, BUT there is something of concern. They showed me the x-ray of my head and a mass the size of a quarter in the middle of the right side of my brain. They said they didn't know what it was but I needed to immediately get a CT scan done and see a neurologist because it did not look good. They gave me the prints and set me up for a CT scan the next morning in Alexandria, LA. Ray was so concerned that he went over with the x-rays to another doctor's house to show them to him. He said to make sure we got this checked out as soon as possible and wished us good luck. I went to church that night and Bro. Lloyd Bustard was preaching. I showed the x-ray to my pastor, Rev. M.

C. Green, and tears came into his eyes. He said to come to the front for prayer when church started. We started having church and my pastor called me to the front to be prayed for. Bro. Bustard looked at the x-rays. He told me that God was going to heal me. He said when he laid his hands on me and prayed for me that it would feel like hot water was poured on top of my head and would go all the way to my feet when God healed me. Well, I had just had the Holy Ghost for 2 weeks and believed everything the preacher said so that is just what I expected to happen. I guess I had not been in the church long enough to doubt. So I raised my hands and as he started to pray with his hands on my head it felt like hot water was poured on my head and covered my whole body all the way to my feet. I knew God had healed me.

I slept all night and went the next morning to get my CT scan. They took the scan and then I had to wait to see the neurologists. I waited a long time after I went in to see him. He left out and finally came back with the other neurologist. He said they had never seen anything like this in all their years of practice. He said it appeared that a mass of some kind was growing there but something had surrounded it and stopped it. He said that they didn't think that it would grow any more but did not know how that happened. He said go home and come back in 6 months for another CT scan just as a precaution and get one every year for the rest of my life. I never went back for about 10 years until another problem called for a CT scan and it still looked the same. It had not grown one bit. I was just in awe that God cared enough about me to heal me of something that could have taken my life.

The next few years of my home life were full of fear and distress. Ray had one girlfriend after the other. One year on his birthday, I had planned a party for him and invited my mom and his and some other people. That afternoon, he said he couldn't come because his girl-friend had cooked a birthday dinner for him and he had to go to it. So I ironed his jeans and shirt and he left. This girl's fiancé had been talking to me outside one of our apartments a few weeks earlier and when Ray drove by and saw us, he stopped the truck and raised his pistol up and shot at us. Neither one of us was hit but we felt the debris from it hitting close to us. We had to go to court over that and he needed her to testify to his plan and of course he got off without any punishment. That was his reason for being with her. So my family came over for his party without him. I just made excuses for him because I was embarrassed to tell them the truth.

Another girlfriend he had was his best friend's wife. When they were found out, she and her husband di-vorced. This girl gave me such a fit because she would call and hang up on me all the time. I mean several times a day. This was before they had caller ID and we had a business to run and I took all the calls. I was getting so stressed out because I would be busy doing paper-work and she would call and interrupt me. So, I called and reported her to the phone company and long story short they cut off her phone for 6 months because she disregarded their warnings to stop. I got beat up over that pretty bad. Later I was at church one night and her mother-in-law (who went to my church) said something about her and I made a comment to her that was repeat-ed to her husband. It wasn't anything bad- just a simple comment. Ray already knew it when I came home from church and he jumped on me and started pulling out handfuls of my hair which was now down to my waste. He pulled out so much of my hair that I had a bald spot on the left side of my head for months and I couldn't wear my hair up or in a ponytail until it grew back.

God brought me through so many dangerous times that I could have been killed. I prayed everyday and fasted a lot. I read my Bible everyday too. I knew I had to keep God close to me. God is the one who was protecting me and I knew I had to have God whether I had Ray or not. I became close friends with a new lady at our church that had recently received the Holy Ghost. In talking to her, I realized we were in the same situations in our home life. Her husband was even more abusive than mine. I started talking to her and trying to encourage her to pray and live for God even in her bad situation. I told her some of the things that had happened with Ray and how God kept me safe and how He gave me the strength to take one day at a time and handle everything that came my way. Little did I know that she was also talking to Ray and before long she had left her husband and Ray rented her an apartment in Shreveport, LA. He bought her a car and started staying with her while he was working there. I remember one night I was at my mother-in-law's house after church and he called and I could hear her giggling in the background. I knew what was going on, but there was nothing I could do about it. I could not believe he called me while he was in the bed with her. I was shaking all over when I got off the phone. She was also telling him some of the things I had told her about me and Ray but she added things to it and he came home and jerked me around and tore my clothes. I only got a black eye that you could see and a small gash by my lip that made it swell up. The rest of the bruises could be hidden under my clothes. I bought some makeup to cover my black eye as much as I could and went on to church. I remember how wonderful it was to be in church that night with Christian people that worshiped God and prayed and sang. We had a prayer line that night and I went through it to be prayed for. I was so desperate for God to help me. His comfort swept over me and calmed me that night and I went on home after church to the dreaded life I lived, but with a feeling of comfort knowing God was going home with me.

Spending time alone with God on my knees in prayer and going to church was my refuge from the life I lived at home. Lots of times, I would leave the house crying with Little Ray headed for church. I couldn't wait to get there. Little Ray saw most of what happened at our house. He didn't say much. He would just go to his room and shut the door. I always told both my kids that when Daddy comes home mad, to go in their room and pray until it was over and to not come out for anything. I was so afraid they would get in the line of fire and get hurt themselves.

Ray decided that it was ok for me to move out so I rented an apartment across town. He would not let me take Little Ray with me so I cried all the time. I got a job at a drug store and his girlfriend came to use the pay phone that was right outside the front door almost every day they were in town. Just seeing her made me want to cry. I stayed in that apartment for 2 months and I decided to go back because I couldn't stand to be without

Little Ray, which was Ray's plan. He didn't think I could make it without him and he knew I wouldn't stay away from our son. He wouldn't let him come to my house. I had to come visit him at Ray's house and only with Ray there. I worried about him constantly that his daddy wouldn't take good care of him or put him off on someone else. Eventually, Ray decided that he wanted me back and he sent her off to another state. He quit drinking for about 6 months and things were pretty good for a while. During that time I became pregnant with our daughter, Kalli. When she was born, I was immediately in love with her too, just like I was with my son. Every decision I made was with my children in mind and is until this day. She was a momma's girl until she was 4 or 5 years old. She loved her daddy too. When she got a little older, he would take her to work with him. Our son was 11 years old when our daughter was born. I cried for 3 days when I found out I was pregnant because I was planning to leave Ray as soon as I thought Little Ray was big enough to take care of himself when I wasn't around. But, I guess God had a different plan for me and my family. I am so thankful that we don't always get what we ask for or what we think we need. My daughter and I have always been close and I don't know what I would have done without her when our lives took a drastic change that I will talk about later.

CHAPTER 5

The Move

In 1991 we did a huge job at Barksdale Air Force Base in Bossier City, LA that changed our lifestyle forever. We stayed in an apartment for 3 months while we completed the job and I did all the paperwork and ran errands. I even went on the job and helped them if need be. We made a lot of money and the opportunity came up to buy a sod farm in Natchitoches, LA, so we bought it. This was always Ray's dream and I wanted to be a part of it. We worked on the farm from before daylight until sometimes midnight. He was out working late almost every night of the week-Sunday was the same as any other day.

I had to drive back and forth from Leesville every-day while Little Ray was in school. Ray put a small trail-er on the farm to stay in while he worked. He and Little Ray would be filthy when they came in and almost too tired to eat. They worked like that for years to make the farm what it is today.

He finally let me handle the money when people would come in and buy sod and he would give me some to spend occasionally too. I started paying my tithes on what he gave me to spend. I always took it out first be-fore I bought anything else as I still do today and God has always, without fail, provided for me. Occasionally, Ray would still go out to the clubs and come home drunk. I was still cautious around him at all times be-cause I never knew what may trigger an outbreak of anger and someone would get hurt. It didn't happen a lot, but when it did, someone would get hurt and some-thing would get destroyed. Even the employees were cautious of him. They too have seen his violent temper outburst especially if something went wrong and it cost him money.

....

We Worked Hard

Things went pretty good for the first few years after buying the sod farm. All we did was work. Ray was at the farm everyday and could outwork any one there…and did. He was intolerant of anyone who did not work hard and long. I have seen them cut grass until after 2 am. One time when Little Ray was about 12 or 13, they had been cutting grass all day long and it was well after midnight and they were still cutting. He told his daddy that he was tired in front of the other employees and when they got home, he hit Little Ray and got him on the floor and started kicking him in the back and stomach. I jumped on him and he threw me off out the front door. The employees stood and watched knowing they had better not say a word. Ray told Little Ray the next morning that he had better never hear him complain in front of the employees again because that would mess up their work. Making money was always the most important thing to him.

The drive to Leesville and back several times a week was getting to be a problem and Big Ray wanted Little Ray to be working. So we started looking for a house to buy. We looked at a lot of them but never found one we really liked. We found some property just outside of town and fell in love with the place. It was very private and had enough acreage that we wouldn't have to worry about close neighbors. We bought it and started looking at house plans.

We had always heard how hard it was on a marriage to build a house, but that was not the case with us. We mostly had the same taste and things went pretty smooth. It took eight months to build our house. We were so anxious to move in before Christmas and that we did. We moved enough of our things in to stay there on Kalli's fifth birthday, two days before Christmas. We didn't have any carpet on the floor and we slept on our mattresses on the floor, but we didn't care. Our house was almost finished and we were so happy to finally have a home on our own. This was such a happy day, or it started out to be. We went to the grocery store to get something for dinner that night and Ray got mad at me about something and he followed me all around the store yelling and cursing me and everybody was staring. He was already drunk before we left. He had been celebrating our new home all day. This event ruined the night for me. I went to bed and turned over and cried. This was supposed to be a special night-our first night in our new home, and he ruined it. We will never have a first night in our first new home again.

We finally finished moving in by the end of the year. It was a beautiful house. It was a story and a half with lots of windows and a three-car garage with a big in-ground pool in the back yard. Ray landscaped it and planted solid sod all over our yard. It was the house we always dreamed of. We had mostly good times over the next couple years, except for the occasional outburst of anger. The serious ones were only happening a couple times a year.

CHAPTER 7

Then He Turned 40

*O*n October 1999 Ray turned 40 years old. I could not believe my eyes when I saw him drive up in a new Corvette. He said he bought it for his birthday. My heart did a flip and fear gripped me when I started thinking about what this could mean. He has had a number of Corvettes since we've been married and it only means one thing---girlfriends! And that is an issue of its own. He always got really mean with me when he had a girlfriend. He gradually started going out to clubs again, sometimes staying out all night. I never asked him where he had been or who he was with because I knew I would be picking myself up off the floor if I did.

In 2000, we bought a house on Toledo Bend. It was a quiet place to go for the weekend to get away from everything. It had a dock and a boat ramp so we bought a boat and a jet ski to have fun. I love to fish and we fished a good bit. We remodeled the inside and the outside and really enjoyed going there and cooking on the grill and relaxing.

Ray always did the cooking at the camp and was an excellent cook. Somehow, everything he cooked always turned out to be perfect. Everybody loved his cooking.

Our camp house finally became a party house. Family and friends would come when we were there. Ray cooked and they all drank beer and played pool. The inside was set up like a pool hall complete with beer signs on the wall (not my choice at all). I incorporated a fishing and hunting theme into the décor as much as I could. People would come on the weekends or on holidays and bring beer and something to throw on the grill. Some would be in the boat or on the Jet Ski and some would be playing pool or volley ball. It started getting out of hand when the people we invited started inviting their friends and family. One time we ended up with over 30 people there and some of them we didn't even know. A couple people even brought their dogs. We finally had to quit having so many parties to get it under control.

One New Year's Eve we had a house full of people. Everyone was drinking and playing pool and dancing and partying. I and my sister were the only two sober people in the house. It was very cold so most everyone was inside except for when they smoked. We did not allow smoking in our house (thank God). Ray had been cooking and the beer fridge had been emptied a couple times so everybody was really messed up. I got the camcorder and filmed the rest of the evening so I could show everybody just how ridiculous they looked. Some were singing and saying and doing things that they would never do sober.

It snowed that night so everybody went down to the dock and shot firecrackers into the water. No one fell in, but I really don't know how. Then they came back at midnight and opened a bottle of champagne to celebrate the New Year and it went all over them. Most of them didn't go to bed until 3 or 4 in the morning so it was the next afternoon when they got up. That night I told them I had something to show them and when they started looking at the video of the night before, they started tucking their heads and getting up and going outside. They didn't want to watch it. I never saw the video again. I don't know who got it, but it disappeared.

I really enjoyed staying at the camp and getting away from the farm. The only thing was that I could only go on Friday and Ray wanted me to stay until Monday morning. He hated for me to go to church and that would make me miss church. I did not like to miss church. Occasionally Kalli and I would go to church close by, but it still wasn't home. I wanted to go home on Saturday night, but Ray would get mad. Sometimes

I would get up and leave on Sunday morning so I could be at my own church. This always made Ray mad and sometimes he would stay an extra night at the camp and not answer the phone. A few times he would get mad and I would stay there to keep trouble down, but he just made me so miserable with his griping and fussing and downing me because I had rather be in church than with him.

He hated the way I dressed and really downed me, even in front of other people, because I didn't wear shorts and bikinis like everyone else did at the lake house. He always said, "Why can't you just go to church on Sundays and be normal the rest of the week." I told him, "There's no need to go at all if you are not going with your whole heart." I needed God every day of the week, not just on Sundays. My life was in God's hands and I did not take living for Him lightly. I prayed every day and studied my Bible every morning. That is what gave me the strength to face my life. Sometimes I would just look up to God and say, "Is this really my life?" Why couldn't I have a husband that loved me for who I am? Why did I have to listen to cursing and vulgar talking all the time and expose my kids to it? Why couldn't my kids have a loving dad like I had?

I always watched out the window while I was praying so I could get busy with something else if I saw Ray coming home. He did not like for me to pray or read my Bible or anything to do with God or church. He always said I should be spending time reading books or studying something that would help us make more money instead of reading foolishness. Sometimes I needed more prayer time than what I could get at home so I would pray that Ray would send me out of town for a part or something so I could get to myself-just me and God. Some of my best prayer times and most refreshing visits with God have been in my car on the road. I would come back a different person with a renewed strength and a half ton lighter from being in the presence of God. It's those times along with my daily praying and reading the Word that has kept me going all these years. Micah 7:8 says,"…When I sit in darkness, the Lord shall be a light unto me." Many times in my life things were so dark I couldn't see my way. Darkness and fear was all around me. I dreaded to see morning come to get up and face the day not knowing what would happen that day. God knew when I was at my wits end and could not go on and He would shine His light on me and refresh my soul and give me strength and encouragement to keep going. I would have never made it this far without God's strength to lift me up. I don't know how people live without God.

CHAPTER 8

What Does It Take?

$\mathcal{R}$ay's mother was getting up in age and started to need more care so we bought a house right down the street from ours for her and her husband to live in so we could check on them more often. We worked on the inside and outside and planted grass all around the house. Ray also built up the driveway and made it a nice place to live. When we first bought it, Ray had our driver to bring the dozer over there to begin work. Ray got up on the dozer that was still on the trailer and cranked it up and it started sliding. He put the brakes on but it still kept sliding off the trailer until it landed on its side in the ditch. I was coming around the curve and saw it all. I stopped and jumped out of my car and ran over there screaming for Ray and praying that he wasn't hurt or dead. When I got to him, he was crawling out of the cage which he had held onto. It was a pure miracle that he wasn't under that machine and crushed. He was shaking so badly he could hardly walk. He made it over to a stump and sat down. All he could say was, "go get me a beer!" I thought, "Are you crazy? How can you think of a beer when God just kept you from getting killed?" He never one time even acknowledged God for saving his life that I ever knew of.

A few years earlier, he had some problems with his feet and legs and was worried about having cancer. His mom and dad both had cancer and he always worried about every ailment being cancer. We went to doctor after doctor to make sure he was getting the right diagnosis. They ran all kinds of tests on him. He was so convinced he had cancer that he started praying and going to church with me. He went to the altar and repented and received the Holy Ghost and was baptized the same night. He started reading his Bible and really changed. He quit drinking and running around. Even the employees and my son said that they could see a change in him. This went on for a couple months and when all the tests came back in with nothing seriously wrong with him, he quit going to church and started going backwards. He never tried to change after that again (that I know of). I fully believe the scripture that talks about when a man turns his back on God that seven devils more evil than the first would enter him (Read Luke 11:24-26). I have witnessed it with my own eyes.

He has been through several close calls even when he was younger. What does it take to wake up some people to realize just who God is and how much control He has on your life? Every time something happened that could have been a tragedy, he would only drink more for several days.

CHAPTER 9

He Gets Worse

After we bought the house for Ray's mother, I noticed he had to go to Leesville a lot. He said he was dealing with a realtor about renting her house. I had no reason to believe otherwise until it just kept going on. I started getting calls that had the number blocked and that only meant one thing- a new girlfriend which, of course, was the realtor. Most of the time they just hung up when I answered, but sometimes they would ask for Ray. If he was there, I gave him the phone and he would get real mad. One time Ray and I was at the camp house and this girl called. I knew who it was even though the number was blocked because of the numerous times she had called before and asked for Ray. So, when I saw who was calling, I handed the phone across the bar to Ray where he was eating dinner and said, "Here, it's for you." He looked at the phone and realized who it was and got so mad he threw the phone at me and hit me in my right side on that bone just below my waist. It hit so hard the phone busted and went all over the floor. Then he threw his glass of milk at me and it burst everywhere. He was standing there yelling at the top of his voice and cursing me for everything he could think of until his face was blood red and the veins were sticking out on his neck. He told me I better get that mess cleaned up quick and fix him another glass of milk, except not in nice words. I was crying and praying under my breath that he would stay on the other side of the bar and not hit me more. That bone was burning and stinging and immediately turned a dark black-purple color and started swelling up. By morning I couldn't wear my fitted clothes because it hurt too much. It took more than 3 weeks for the swelling to go down and the pain to ease up enough to wear my fitted clothes. I always wondered if it didn't chip off a piece of the bone that day because it took a long time to heal completely. As I was cleaning up the milk and glass and phone pieces off the floor, he had started eating the rest of his dinner. He had food and milk all in his beard and he could barely keep his eyes open because he was so drunk. He had his .357 magnum pistol lying on the bar beside him and he put his hand on it. It was pointed in my direction. I was still praying under my breath the whole time and praying the gun would not go off. I would glance over at the gun every few minutes and could see his finger on the trigger with the hammer pulled back. I would watch as his finger tightened up on the trigger and then let loose and kept it pointed at me as I cleaned up the mess. I just kept praying that God would protect me, but that if it did go off and I was killed, that there would not be any sin in my life that would keep me from going to Heaven. I just kept thinking, "I've got to have you, God. I know you will either keep me safe or take me to a better place." Sometimes I would even pray to God and ask Him to see that my children had someone to care for them that would teach them about Him and take them to church and care for them like I would if something did happen to me.

Well, God did not allow Ray to even pick the gun up off the counter that night. I could see his hand gripping it and squeezing the trigger, but God stepped in. I believe with all my heart that Ray could not pull the trigger or even pick up the gun that night. God would not let him. Do you think it pays to live for God? You tell me!

I started praying that God would not let me get in a situation with Ray where the only way out was to kill him. I didn't want to kill him and him end up in Hell and I didn't want to be put in a situation where I had to kill him to protect me or my kids. Thank God it never came to that.

My body finally healed. My heart, however, never healed. This is a Christian book and I could never write the words Ray said to me over the years and how much they hurt. If you can imagine the worst language used on the street and in rated R and X movies, that is the way my husband talked to me. He called me every name that came to his mind and even made up names and used God's name in vain. He had a very vulgar and perverted language that he used around me and Little Ray. Sometimes I wondered why God put up with that. It was bad enough the way he treated me, but some of the language used with God's name in it was repulsive. I always had to get away and pray afterwards and clean out my mind and my thoughts of all the ugliness I just heard. I also had to ask God to help me forgive and love the way a wife should, but it was getting harder every day. I was not going to let him send me to hell by having an unforgiving spirit or holding a grudge. I knew I had to get right because I never knew what day might be my last. I tried so hard to do everything right because I didn't want to be the one to provoke him to curse God. Sometimes I would have to pray for several days to feel the release of forgiveness to move on to the next day. He never apologized about any of his angry outbursts because he said I caused him to do it. He always said I shouldn't make him so mad and I wouldn't get hurt. He always expected me to get up the next day and act like nothing ever happened. If he got up in a loving mood, I had better be in one too and not half-heartedly either or it would start all over again. I would be so glad when he would leave for work even though I never knew when he might come back. Once he left, I would just melt on the floor in my dining room in the arms of Jesus, my best friend, and at times my only friend. (I always prayed in the dining room so I could see if he came up the driveway.) I couldn't tell my friends or my family the details of my life. We were business people in this town and liked and respected by most people. A few of my close friends knew a little about my life but not the details.

One night after I came home from church he got mad at Little Ray about something he said that he didn't like. It was no big deal, but it hit him the wrong way. He jumped up and started chasing Little Ray around the house with his pistol pointed at him and calling him names and cursing him and threatening to kill him. When Little Ray came through the living room, he jumped over the rocking chair by the fireplace and almost broke his toe, but he never slowed down. He ran out the door with his dad on his heels and took off down the driveway with nothing on but his shorts and it was ice cold outside. His dad started shooting at him because he couldn't run any more. I was crying and praying and screaming at Ray to leave him alone. Little Ray stayed out by the mailbox for a long time until he felt like he could come back. He didn't come back up the driveway until his dad started yelling out to come back in that he would not hurt him. Ray calmed down and let Little Ray back in the house on a promise that he would not hurt him. The whole end of his toe was raw and bleeding so I doctored it and we went to bed for the night. God stepped in again and did not let anyone get killed. I have been physically hurt many times just as Little Ray has and it all eventually heals. It's the words that don't heal as quickly. It has taken me years to get past them. They hurt deeper than any physical pain you can imagine. All this really caused my love for Ray to dry up and almost die. Every time he would take his anger out on me or the kids, it killed a little more love each time, especially when it was the kids.

CHAPTER 10

God, I Can't Take It Any More!

By 2001, I was so nervous all the time just trying to stay ahead of any angry outbreaks that might happen because by now he had started mixing alcohol with drugs. Anything that happened with the farm or concerning our kids that might be a trigger point, I tried to hide it at all cost if I could. I did not want anything to make him mad if I could help it. I took the blame for a lot of things my kids did and covered for them because I couldn't stand it when Ray hurt them. I had rather he hurt me. I had no self-esteem at all so I never gave my opinion about anything unless I was asked and even then I knew what kind of answer I should give.

Everything I did was not good enough to suit him. He always said he was going to get someone to work in the office that would do things just like he wants them done. I knew that would never happen. He would have to pay them and I worked for free. Besides, I always did things just the way he said even if I didn't agree because I knew the consequences if I didn't. He could find something wrong with anything and everybody. That's just the way he was. He never saw the good in things, always the bad. He could find the bad in something even if he had to dig for it. Sometimes he would point out the bad in something and I would sit and wonder, "How did he come up with that?"

I loved the farm life and enjoyed the business, but I hated working for him because he did so many things that were not right. I prayed over everything that I had to turn in that it would not come back on me. He always said that you can't get ahead in business if you go by the law. Finally, I started praying one day after one of Ray's threats to hire someone to take my place. I asked God to help me get totally out of our business because I did not want to be a part of any wrongdoings any more. I asked him to let Ray say that he wanted to get someone to help me in the office if it was His Will to do so. Then I could gradually work my way out of doing the things I didn't want to do. Within a few weeks he said he wanted to build a new office on the farm and put someone out there to help me and I could still work here in my office at home. God had heard my prayer and was making some changes for me. He saw my desperation to get out of being a part of his wrongdoings so he opened the door and started working. I just didn't know how much my life was going to change in the next few years. This was just the beginning.

Ray hired a girl to work at the farm and I would still work in my office at the house. She worked there until she couldn't take his foolishness any more. He wanted her to lie for him and cover his phone calls and she didn't want to be in the middle.

Then I hired a new girl in the spring of 2002. I spent a good bit of time with her to make sure she would know everything about the business. I also told Ray to tell her how to do some things that I knew were not right because I didn't want to be a part of anything wrong.(I didn't dare tell him that). Besides that, it was Ray she had to please. Ray had no idea of my plan to get away from the business. I could never let him even think that. I also enrolled in a local college to further my education for the time I may need to get a job if I got on my own. Ray agreed to let me go to school now that I had help so I could be a better bookkeeper.

I never blamed the girl for covering for him because I knew she was just following orders. Ray continued to party and have girlfriends and things got worse between us. I don't know why he became so mean to me when he would have a girlfriend. That was the tell-tale sign of what was happening. When he would act like that, all I had to do was just start paying attention to things and he eventually would tell off on himself.

He would start making negative comments about what I was wearing or not wearing as the case may be or talking about how I was brain-washed into believing that you need to go to church so much. He would get mad at the drop of a hat for no reason. Sometimes he would get mad and start blaming me for things I had nothing to do with or even knew about. Next thing I knew he would be so mad that he would grab me and pick me up by my collar and hold me to the wall while he cursed and threatened or worse; sometimes with a pistol in his hand. One night he got so mad at me he hit the kitchen table so hard that the end broke off. That made him even madder so he picked up one of the chairs and threw it at me. I dodged it and it knocked a hole in the wall. He sent me to the furniture store the next day to buy a new table and two new chairs. I also went and bought some caulking and fixed the hole in the wall and repainted it the best I could and put a small table in front to cover it.

One night I had already gone to bed and was asleep. He came in very late and was so drunk he could barely walk. His stumbling through the house is what woke me up. He came in the bedroom and jumped up on the bed and straddled me. He picked up the pistol that was lying by the bed and put it right up to my mouth and pulled the hammer back. He started saying how he hated the way his mom brought him up and made him go to church. (She lived the life everyday that would put my prayer life to shame.) He said he always told himself when he was growing up that he would get away from that life and didn't want to have any part of it the rest of his life and he said, "and I'll be a monkey's uncle* if I didn't marry someone just like her." *(language changed) He was shaking all over and I was praying under my breath that God would keep that gun from going off. He eventually calmed down and laid the pistol down and went on to bed. I never did know what triggered that outbreak, but it scared me to think of what he thought about God.

CHAPTER 11

Praying And Fasting

Eventually Ray started looking at our daughter, Kalli with his evil eyes. He had a stare that he would give when he was really drunk or drugged up that made you think he was thinking something awfully evil about you; maybe to hurt you or something. He looked at me like that quite often, but now that he was looking at her like that, I knew I had to do something. I started praying and fasting and seeking guidance from God as I could without his knowing about it. He didn't like for me to pray and fast because praying took time away from my work and fasting would starve my brain cells so I couldn't be alert to work the business (in his words). He had no clue that both of them helped me even to handle the business better. He would get mad if he knew I prayed and fasted. I needed to know what to do. Leaving had never been an option because I knew I would never get out alive. Now I am thinking if I don't get away from him, he may hurt Kalli and I could not live with that. I prayed and fasted for about a year looking for answers. God would speak to me through His Word and through other people (even though no one knew the whole situation). He used my pastor, Bro. James Whitehead to give me guidance even though he didn't even know the situation in detail.

Back in 2001, a minister came to our church and prophesied over me. I wrote his words down in a journal so I could write down things as they happened. His exact words are as follows:

July 29, 2001
Sunday Morning
"The lady in the peach dress is in need of confirmation of God's will for her life. She is in dire need of deliverance of oppression that comes against her. There is a spiritual gift given unto her, a spiritual sign, not just a gift, but a spiritual anointing in her life that she possesses and the enemy fears her and fears the intercession God has given her in her ministry, in her prayer ministry. She has never been able to fully get to the top of the mountain to view and see what

God wants to do. This morning, believe it or not, by the time she walks to the front of this building there will be over 18 different oppressions that will fall off of her this morning. Her gift ministry of prayer is going to be tuned this morning and is going to begin to work. God is going to answer within 17 days 3 of her prayer requests and it's going to build her faith. Unbelievable! God says there's a turn of events that is about to happen by His hand that God's gonna give her power over every legal move in her life that comes against her that she has to make over the next 3 years. God's hand is with her! She will speak in a language this morning she has never spoken. It will be a new anointing that will break upon her. She will no longer misunderstand the oppression, but she will understand the oppression and God will send her especially to women who have been divorced and are split and are going thru troubles in marriages. And there is an anointing of victory given to her in this area in which she shall minister. And God is going to give her favor to bring people to the house of God and God's going to show her how to witness and to bring people to Him. Now this is going to happen."

Sunday Morning-End of Service

He called me again to the front and said, *"It's time for paybacks isn't it. Huh? You watch. You're not going to have any breakdown. Look at me. Hold your eyes up and look at me. I can tell you right now. You are so chosen of God and so gifted of God. That's why the enemy has went against you. That's why things that you thought would work out haven't worked out because the enemy has been against you. Now, wait until after tonight. Wait until after I preach tonight. You're gonna be able to know and direct as these enemies come against you. You're gonna be able to not just sit there and take them as they come. God doesn't want his church to board up when the hurricane comes. He wants us to stand out there and direct that hurricane. And that's what's gonna happen to you. You're gonna start standing your ground. You're gonna start speaking utterances of the Holy Ghost and when those hurricanes start coming, you're gonna laugh and say, "Uhn uhn, it's too late. God has revealed some things to me and I'm not going to take that anymore". And all these words that are like darts all around you. I see them. They have been piercing you thru the years, every one of them, when I lay hands on you are gonna fall on the ground and shrivel up and die and have no effect on you."*

My Answers

God did answer 3 prayers in 17 days as I wrote in my journal along with numerous other things that happened by the hand of God, just like he prophesied. I wrote in my journal on September 26, 2001 the following about what was prophesied over me:

"God has definitely taken away all of the oppression and depression in my life. I no longer feel that I don't have any control over my life, that there is no way I could ever go to Heaven or be called a Christian in the true sense of the word even though circumstances

have not changed much. I now feel hope inside. I feel that God is in total control of my life and if I keep praying and searching for God's will and only His will and follow His guidance day by day that in my feeble understanding, God will lead me and guide me to make the right decisions in everything that affects my life. I totally trust God and have great faith that He will work out every situation in my life that I can obey Him and work on the calling God has placed on my life that I feel working stronger than ever before.

I have always felt the call of prayer and intercession on my life. I've had the Holy Ghost for 17+ years but I've never felt the liberty and the freedom in prayer like I've felt the last few months. God's presence is so strong immediately when I start to pray. Worship just flows when I pray. All during the day I feel God's presence and have the mind of prayer and the urge to tell God how wonderful He is, and yet I have done a better job of doing my work than ever before.

I have stood my ground the last few weeks about being faithful to attend church regularly. Ray says Sunday night is enough and I told him that "you are wasting your time going at all if you are not doing it wholeheartedly. My goal is to go to Heaven and not attend church as a social event". He just said, "Whatever" and hung up on me then stayed an extra night at the camp, but has been in a good mood since he came home."

As weeks and months went by, I did not dwell on the prophecy that was spoken over my life, but I continued to pray and fast and seek God. I had to make sure that I was doing the right thing and that God was with me or I could be hurt or killed. After all, there aren't many days go by that you don't hear of a woman getting killed or severely beaten up by her husband. A year went by and I was still seeking for an answer.

I had to have a reason with evidence to back it up as to why I needed to leave. The fact of his numerous girlfriends and violent behavior was not good enough. I prayed for God to show me exactly what was going on because I didn't have any concrete evidence of anything to signal me to leave. Then things just started happening. I found different things in his pocket or his wallet or in his truck. He never knew of what I found, but it made me surer of the fact that I needed to get out. I found phone bills and pictures. Once, I went with another sister in the church to Prayer Conference in St. Louis, MO. We were gone for 3 or 4 days. When I got home, I found a girl's wallet with pictures and a beer bottle with lipstick on it down by the pool. I also found a ponytail holder by the pool too. I knew immediately who they belonged to- our newspaper girl (who is younger than our son). I knew when I left that he would carry on with his girlfriend, but I really never thought he would bring her to my house. But I wasn't going to let that keep me home. He would be seeing her whether I went or not. I needed to go to that prayer conference. I needed an answer from God. I was still afraid to go on my own for fear that God was not pleased with the idea of divorce. I knew that divorce was not of God, but then neither was living in fear and danger. I still prayed and fasted and found more things which told me God was showing me what I needed to know to make the decision I had to make. One evening Ray was at home and called from the house phone to check his messages on his cell phone. This was definitely by God's hand because he never did that. When he left, I got his security code off the phone and that was all the information I needed. I listened to his voice mails and found out he didn't only have the one girlfriend that I had found in the pictures, but he indeed had another one, possibly two more. Over the next couple years his own voice mail would be my main instrument of knowing the truth. He never knew what and how I found out until this day.

In The Washroom

I kept praying for guidance and wisdom to make the right decision in leaving because I knew if it was not the right one, I could end up hurt or even dead. I had to know God was with me and that He had a new plan for me. I also knew that I was affecting my kid's life by my decisions and I didn't want Kalli to keep being afraid everyday of her daddy coming home. He never tried to hurt her, but she was afraid of what he would do to me. Little Ray had already moved out by then.

I had been asking God for signs all along to make me to know that I was in His Will and that He did have another plan for my life. I know asking for signs makes you think "doubt" but I never doubted God. I doubted myself and my ability to know if God was telling me something or if I was so anxious to have a plan that I would do the wrong thing thinking it was God. I was so afraid of making the wrong decision that could cost me my life and my children's life. Finally, I asked God that if it was part of His plan for me to leave, then let Ray bring it up. I knew it was next to impossible for him to want me to leave. He would never allow that. I took care of everything and still brought in the money. He could be gone as long as he wanted and he knew everything would be taken care of. I would be there selling the sod and booking deliveries and Little Ray would take care of everything in the field. If he mentioned that we should spend time apart, it would definitely be of God.

I was in the wash room ironing that evening and he came in there to talk. We talked about how we were pulling apart from each other and that we needed to do something. He asked me what I thought we should do and I told him I didn't know. Then he asked me what I thought about us spending a little time away from each other just to get ourselves together and give us time to think about what we need to do. He said he would get an apartment for a while and I could stay in the house. When he said those words, my heart jumped up in my throat and started pounding. I knew I just got my answer from God and now it was my turn to move on it. I was so afraid. I was glad for the answer but sad that it had come to this. We were both crying and I really thought that he was going to work on our marriage too. I told him I would get an apartment and he could stay in the house (because I did not want him to be coming in and out as he wanted to).

The next day I started looking for an apartment to rent and found one. I came home and told him what I had found and he had already changed his mind. He said there was no need to go that I needed to stay and we would just try to work it out. He said he wasn't seeing anybody and wanted to make things right with me. BUT, I knew I had a word from the Lord when he answered my prayer like He did and I could not go back on it. It would be too dangerous for me to stay after God had made a way of escape. So I told him that we had an agreement and that it would be good for us to be apart for a while to sort things out. So, I rented the apartment and started packing. He didn't want me to take any furniture so he told me to go buy new furniture and he would pay for it. I only packed what I needed to keep house because I was so sure Ray would come to his senses and not give up his family of 25 years for alcohol, drugs and girlfriends. Even in all his meanness, I still loved him to a certain degree because I had been with him since I was 15 years old even though I sometimes had to pray for God to help me not to hate him when he would do things to me and my children. I knew he had an alcohol and drug problem and that made him a completely different person. It was bad enough when he was drunk, but when he mixed pills with his beer and mixed drinks, it changed his whole personality. He was a fun and likable person when he was sober and we enjoyed a lot of the same things.

CHAPTER 13

The Night We Left

I left with Kalli to spend our first night in our apartment on September 25, 2002. She had a slumber party to go to so I actually spent it alone. I never got afraid of being alone that night and slept good even though I was sad that it had to come to this. As I started telling my family and friends of our separation, all they could say was, "Are you nuts? Are you going to leave that beautiful house and all the things you worked for all these years and let him have them and give them to his girlfriend?" They did not understand because I had not told anyone the horrible details of our life. I was willing to move out and live in a mobile home and drive an old jalopy if I could go to sleep at night and not be afraid. Some understood my thinking after I told them some of the details but some don't understand even today how I could leave everything behind.

I was already going to school by now and it was hard to get up and go with all that was going on. I could hardly eat anything. I nibbled on peanut butter crackers while I was going to school. I was sick at my stomach most of the time knowing this could be the end of my marriage. I know it was only the hand of God that helped me to graduate with a 99.7 GPA with 2 business degrees. I never thought for a moment that we would be permanently apart. I was so sure that Ray would give up the drugs and alcohol that made him the violent person he had become and that my love and loyalty to him for 25 years would stand out enough to him to get rid of all his girlfriends. But, I was wrong. I listened everyday to his voicemail messages because I knew it would not lie. While he was telling me every day that he didn't have a girlfriend and didn't want one and he only wanted me, his voicemail told a different story. One day he had come over to my apartment and stayed a while. We talked about things and I thought maybe we could work on this. About an hour after he left my apartment, I checked his voicemail and his girlfriend had left him a message that said she hated that she missed his phone call that she was on her route (the newspaper girl) but that she loved him too. Her message was just minutes after he left my house. Again, my heart broke. Why was I not enough for him? How could you spend over 25 years with someone and give up your whole life with them for someone else-especially since she was younger than our son. I wanted him to love me and for us to grow old together. I wanted him to quit all his drinking and drugs and get a handle on his angry outbursts. He was a totally different person when he wasn't on that mixture and we liked to do a lot of the same things. But, by this time he was messed up more than he was sober.

By the way, I lucked up and what would you know, the apartment I rented was right on his girlfriend's route. She brought me my newspaper everyday too.

CHAPTER 14

My Last Trip Home

A couple weeks after I moved out, I realized that things were not going to change so I decided that I would go back to our house and get some more of my things. I called Ray and told him that I would come over after church and would appreciate it if he would see that his girlfriend and he be gone. He said ok, so I went. Kalli had gone home with a friend, thank God. I pulled up in the drive and his girlfriend's car was in the carport, His truck was gone so I went on in the house with my boxes. I set my boxes on the floor and looked up to see his girlfriend coming out of the bedroom with a cleaning rag in her hand. She immediately turned around and went back in the bedroom and shut the door, then went out the back door from the bedroom and got in her car and left. That was the first time I had ever actually seen her in MY house. I walked into our bedroom and saw HER things on MY nightstand. I was shaking all over and crying as I opened a couple of my dresser drawers and her things were in them. My things had been put in the corner of my walk-in closet where her things now hung. I started crying uncontrollably. Could I have been such a failure of a wife to lose everything we had together for a young girl? I walked back in the kitchen and started loading my boxes and Ray drove up. I was still crying, feeling cheated and mad and hurt all at the same time and I was still shaking severely all over. I was up on a ladder getting some of my things from the top shelf when he came in. I could tell right away that he was really messed up. He casually walked in with his hands in his pocket and we started talking. He said a couple things and I let loose on him. I could not stop telling him about my hurt and confusion and anger and everything else I was feeling and had felt the last few months. I never said anything ugly or that I regret. I was just telling him my heart. I was crying hard and shaking uncontrollably all over. He told me to get down off the ladder that I was going to fall and hurt myself, but the words just kept coming as I packed my things. Finally I got down and moved the ladder over to the fireplace to get down a picture that was hanging over the mantle. I climbed up the ladder and he eased up behind me and said, "Are you ready to die?" My heart jumped up in my throat as I turned around and said, "I don't want to die today." He said, "Well you'd better get ready because me and you both are fixing to die right now. I'm going to kill you and then kill myself. This just ain't worth it." About that time I heard the hammer click on his pistol as he pulled it back-still in his pocket. He was shaking all over just like I was and looking at me through glassy, bloodshot eyes. As I was praying under my breath for God to step in and take control and guide my words to say the right thing, I calmly talked to him and said, "Ray, you may kill me today. But when I stand before God, I'll be going to a better place. What will God say to you when you face Him? Do you think He is going to let you into Heaven? You don't really want to face God today do you?" I kept talking in that manner to him (still praying under my breath) for what seemed like eternity and I heard the hammer click again releasing it down. I felt weak all over knowing what almost happened. My legs were shaking so badly I could hardly get off the ladder. Ray started crying. He walked to the table and sat down and laid the pistol on the table. He put his face in his hands and started saying, "I can't believe what I almost did. I can't believe what I almost did. Kim, you got to pray for me. I almost pulled the trigger on both our lives." I told him that I prayed for him every day. I could barely walk I was shaking so badly but I gathered the boxes and things I had already packed and loaded them in my car and left. I went to my apartment and fell on the floor sobbing and thanking God for taking care of me that day once more. I was weak as a rag and all I could do was move my lips, but God understood every word. I spent the rest of the afternoon until church time with my face on the floor before God and in His presence where I found comfort and safety. His loving arms held me tight that afternoon and made me to know how much He loved and cared about me. I never went back and got anything else after that.

The next few months were full of fear and depression as to the outcome of my future. Even though you have a word from God, uncertainty can drain you. I started going to a Christian family psychologist for counseling because I could not get a hold of myself. I felt like I was not pleasing God because I gave up on my marriage and maybe if I had toughed it out a little longer, God could have used me to get through to Ray. I knew God had made a way for me to escape, but I still blamed myself for giving up. The counselor helped me to see that this marriage was in default ever since he first cheated on me in our first year of marriage. He gave me scriptures and literature to help me to understand that it is not God's plan for his children to live in fear and that I could not fix this situation on my own. He helped me to see that God was not going to hold me accountable for a marriage based on lies, violence and adultery and that God actually wanted me to be free of that life. After several weeks of counseling I started to feel less guilt and feel more relief.

CHAPTER 15

Fear Turns To Bitterness

ight after night and day after day my mind was consumed by the thoughts of how hard I worked for the things I left, that the house we had built was now enjoyed by someone else and I had a small apartment, that the car I had was an old car from our business and that she now drove my new car that he had gotten me for Christmas the year before, was sleeping in my bed, etc. and I was having to start my life over. We had talked about retiring in a few years, but now I had to get a new job and it would be at least twenty more years before I could think of retiring. These things eat on me every waking hour. I don't know how I managed to keep my grades up. Except for the help of God I would not have made it. These thoughts turned into bitterness and that is the strongest leach I have ever dealt with in my life. Bitterness will not let you go. Bitterness will make you have a negative attitude all the time. Bitterness will consume your life to where you think of nothing else. Finally, my pastor's wife gave me a book called, "How to Forgive when It's Hard to Forget" by Joy Haney. That book changed my life. It showed me that I had let bitterness overtake my life to the point that I had basically made a shrine to it, like I had started to worship it. It was on my mind so much I couldn't even think about God or anything else. Letting myself think about it all the time made it a god in my life. Those words were a real eye-opener for me. So, I repented with a broken heart for letting this come between me and God. I never wanted anything to take the place of God in my life, certainly not a past hurt that I could do nothing about.

I started healing over my bitterness. It was a long, hard road to beat, but I finally got victory over it. It took me about a year to get over being bitter through a lot of prayer and fasting and reading the Word and then, my bitterness turned into thanksgiving. I realized that I can't look back at the past and what it should have been, but that I now was to look forward to the new plan God had for my life.

CHAPTER 16

Divorce... Or Not?

I had been gone about six months and decided I might as well file for divorce and get it over with and maybe Kalli and I could move on with our lives. This is what I wrote in my journal:

March 19, 2003

My "legal moves" are about to begin. I can hardly believe this is happening after being married 24 years.

I always thought Ray would grow out of his partying lifestyle and his need for girlfriends. I thought that my love and dedication to him and our business would count for something by now and he would know that I love him with all my heart. I have never put anything else above him in my life. I was only going to church part-time and half-heartedly living for God. I knew I wasn't right but I also knew that a marriage was meant to last forever and I could not have both. But, with all I've been through with Ray, I realize that God is the one in control of my life. God is the one that says if I live or die, by Ray's hand or other means. I can't turn my back on God for Ray. Ray has plainly showed me that his love for me is not real. God has made a way for me to really see what Ray is and he does not "love" me like a husband of 24 years should. He needs me because I know his routines and what he likes and don't like and he knows he can depend on me to handle everything that he doesn't want to and see that everything goes smooth while he is gone. I see, after 6 months of separation, that he is not going to quit drinking but only get worse. He is not going to give up his girlfriends either. I feel that God has delivered me safely from a bad situation because Ray has no desire to change. My heart is broken over the fact that we will not be together anymore because I love him with all my heart and I guess I always will. I thank God for what he is doing in my life. I can only trust God to help me make the right decisions in every part of my life and follow the plan he has for me."

I was scared to death to mention divorce to him because all he would see is that I would be trying to take

HIS stuff (mostly his money that I helped him work for). I looked in the phone book for a lawyer that I knew he was not friends with and have never heard him speak of. I knew that if I went to one of them that was friends with him, they might not take my case because they knew he had the money and then tell him that I was enquiring about a divorce. I was a nervous wreck. I finally found one that was unfamiliar to me and gave him a call. I went to his office in a nervous frenzy and hurried to park in the back so Ray wouldn't see my car if he drove by. I only wanted a house to live in, a car to drive me to work, and a little income to supplement my job so Kalli and I could live comfortably. Ray could have the rest if he would just leave me alone. Everyone thought I was crazy to give up all the things we had acquired to him, but I didn't want to live in fear any more. If I tried to take "my half", he would surely have me killed. His whole life was consumed with money.

I had my lawyer to draw up the papers to file for divorce. I knew it would infuriate Ray to be served in front of the employees or his girlfriend, so I told the lawyer I would call Ray and tell him to pick up the papers at the courthouse. I was so nervous about making that call. I was shaking all over as I dialed the phone not knowing what would happen when I told him. Just like I thought, HE WAS MAD! He started cursing me and calling me all kinds of names and telling me that I was going to come up missing along with numerous other threats. I hung up on him.

Ray was supposed to pick up Kalli that night to spend the weekend with him and I was scared to death for him to come over. He called me numerous times that afternoon with all kinds of threats on my life. He said he had some mafia friends that would take care of me, that I would come up missing and no one would ever find anything but pieces and that they were there with him while we were talking. He said they would put me in the trunk and take me off and gang rape me and then kill me and no one would ever know what happened to me. He said that I was writing the final chapter of my life and it was up to me how it ended. He ended by saying he was not picking Kalli up and then slammed the phone down. In a few minutes he called to say that he was picking Kalli up and that he was on his way. My stomach was in knots. I was not afraid of him hurting Kalli-he had never threatened her. I was only afraid of his irresponsible behavior around her and that in the end she might get hurt. I was also afraid of what he might do to me when he got to my house. I gave Kalli a hug and told her that I loved her and sent her out the door when he pulled up. I stood in the door not wanting to get any closer. He motioned for me to come closer to his truck, so I went out a few steps. Then he motioned again for me to come even closer. I slowly walked to his truck. My legs were weak as a dishrag and I was shaking all over as I proceeded toward the truck where he sat. Kalli had already gotten in the truck with him. I got just out of range where he couldn't reach me and stopped. He stared at me for a minute and then said, "I just wanted to look at you one more time." He had that glassy stare in his eyes that made me quiver, like he was thinking some terrible thoughts about me. Then he backed out of my driveway and left. I went back inside and locked the door and started praying. I didn't know what he had on his mind or what his plans were, but I knew I needed God to intervene. I prayed that God would protect Kalli and bring her back home safely. I also prayed for protection for myself. I went in every room of the house and anointed each door and window with oil and pleaded the blood of Jesus over me and my house. I prayed that if anyone came to my house to hurt me that they would see angels surrounding my house and would leave me alone. I went to bed and slept all night.

Ray sent Kalli home the next day and I asked about her visit. She said nothing bad happened and that she had a good time. I discretely asked about the trip to his house from my house because I did not want to alarm her or make her afraid. She said when they left my house that he called somebody from his cell phone and said, "She is home alone now" and hung up. Then they went home and he made another phone call but she didn't hear what was said. Then he left her at the house with his girlfriend and was gone for a while.

I still, to this day, do not know what was about to happen that night, but I know without a doubt that God sent His angels to watch over me. I did not pursue getting the divorce any further at this time.

After living in the apartment for several months and still listening to Ray's voicemail, I realize the hope of Ray changing and us being back together was getting smaller and smaller. I guess I thought that time would bring him to his senses and he would go back to being the old Ray that I loved. I didn't know what would happen next. I thought Ray might do something that would leave me with nothing, so I decided I would look for a house to buy. I was headed over to look at a house in town when I spotted his girlfriend getting out of her car. When she got out, I saw her big belly…this was when I found out she was pregnant. There is no way to tell you of the hurt I felt at that moment. To think that my husband of 25 years would have a baby with someone else was more than my mind could take. But eventually I got over that too.

Ray ended up buying the house for me and Kalli and I moved in. It was in September 2003. We painted and fixed it just like we wanted it. I tried to make our house a home, even though it was just me a Kalli. I wanted us to have a happy, loving home to share and be safe and secure with each other. Kalli and I became best friends during our time of family tragedy. We always sat on the couch, arm in arm, and watched movies and ate junk food. Sometimes she would come and sleep with me in my bed. She used to like to cook for me too. God knew what He was doing when He gave her to me. She would be my strength to go on.

Thanksgiving came in a few short months. I wanted to have the kids over for dinner like we always did and I decided that I would invite Ray to come so he could be with the kids too. Everybody was nervous about us all getting together. I had cooked all their favorites and we sat down to eat. We were about half way through eating when my home phone rang. The caller ID said "Natchitoches Hospital" so I answered it. The woman's voice on the other line asked if Ray was there and could she speak to him. I asked who was calling and she said her name. It was Ray's girlfriend's mom. She wanted to tell Ray that she was in labor and could he come to the hospital. He told her he would be there in a minute and hung up. The room was perfectly silent. No one said a word. One by one they got up and went outside. No one eat another bite. Ray got up and went to his truck and downed a beer and came back in and said he had to leave. The kids didn't know what to say. Little Ray left and Kalli and I washed all the dishes and went to my mom's house to stay the rest of the week.

CHAPTER 17

Grandma Again???

I was having a Christmas party for the ladies of my church at my house a couple weeks later and one of the elderly ladies congratulated me on being a grandmother again. I told her that I had not had any more grandchildren, but she told me she read about it in the paper. I had been too busy getting ready for the party to read the paper that day so I picked it up and read for myself the article she was talking about. I eased down the hall to my bedroom and shut the door and got myself together so I could finish the party without spoiling it for anyone. The article told of my husband (by name) and his girlfriend (also by name) having a baby and the details about her birth with a picture. I held myself together pretty good until the party was over and then I fell apart. I called Ray and told him how ashamed and embarrassed I was that this was published for all our friends and business acquaintances to see. I asked him how much more he was going to humiliate me. Now EVERYBODY knows! I was crying and screaming at him over the phone. I finally hung up on him and went to bed. In the next few weeks I was in the grocery store and ran into our accountant. She congratulated me also on being a grandmother again. She had seen the article in the paper and thought it was my son too. She could have crawled in a hole when I told her the story and so could I. I was so embarrassed…and so was she.

CHAPTER 18

Still Searching

O n January 2004 I write in my journal:
January 10, 2004
"*I have been praying for direction in my life and what I should do about my marriage to Ray. I feel like divorce is the next step but when I think about it I feel afraid because of the threats made last year when we talked about it. And I am also worried about his cutting us off and not giving me my part-not really my part- but my house and car and financial support for us. I was reading my Bible this*

morning in Genesis, chapter 31 and when I got to verse 38 God said, "Pay attention". Jacob had served Laban in order to marry his daughters and Laban did not want to release him to go back to his homeland with his wives and children and other things he had acquired over the last 20 years. He had been his faithful servant. Jacob reminded Laban, who had cheated his wages, that it was only the mercy of God on his life that let him have what he had because Laban would have give him nothing. God blessed Jacob by letting Laban agree to let him go and also make an oath not to hurt him.

When I read this God reminded me that He would do the same for me as prophesied July 29, 2001. This scripture confirmed that! The prophet said things would change in my life by the hand of God and that I would have power over every legal move in my life. I thank God that he reminds us of His promises to us and reassures us that everything will work our right."

But, I was still afraid to go to a lawyer. I don't know why God come thru for me like he did. He gave me so many assurances and yet I was still afraid. Thank you Jesus for being patient with me!

CHAPTER 19

I Must Have Lost My Mind!

The next year in my life was a disaster...of my own making. Due to some major bad judgment, I let an unspeakable and shameful occurrence happen in my life and was totally unaware of just how big of a disaster it really was. I got took big time. The details are so horrible before God even though I was partly in the blind, I don't even want to share them with you. (I know those wheels are turning now). But, I can tell you that I now can totally relate to and have a sympathetic heart for lonely, hurting women. My heart goes out to them and the struggles they face no matter what the age. It has given me an understanding as to why people make the decisions they make sometimes, even when they know better. Oh God, how could I let such a thing happen in my life? Why didn't I see this coming? I am the church ladies leader. I sing in the praise team. People depend on me to pray and fast and lead. How could I ever let this happen? Oh God, how can you forgive me? I did not plan it this way. I felt so bad that I cried all the time. I became depressed wanting God to forgive me, but I couldn't forgive myself so I didn't feel worthy for God to forgive me. I cried through every church service. I hardly talked to anyone. I would come and sing on the platform-feeling so rotten and hypocritical- and leave as soon as they said the last "amen". I was so ashamed even though no one knew. It was months before I could forgive myself enough to really trust God to forgive me and move on with the life God had planned for me. "It is of the Lord's mercies that we are not consumed because his compassions fail not. They are new every morning: great is thy faithfulness." (Lamentations 3: 22-23) Also, "For we have not an high priest which cannot be touched with the feelings of our infirmities; but was in all points tempted like as we are, yet without sin. Let us therefore come boldly unto the throne of grace that we may obtain mercy, and find grace to help in time of need."(Hebrews 4: 15-16) God really spoke to me through these scriptures and assured me that He understood and forgives.

God eventually, thru a lot of prayer and fasting, healed me of my wrong and helped me put it in the past. I would like to forget it all and act like it never happened, but God taught me a lot of lessons from this one instance that I will never forget. It has helped me to have compassion on other ladies and not be so judgmental of the decisions they make in life and instead, hold them up in prayer. It also showed me that NO ONE is exempt from the snares of the devil. We must be always on guard.

CHAPTER 20

My Kids

*D*uring this time, Big Ray was telling me that Little Ray was in real bad shape taking drugs. He lived and worked on the farm so they were together every day. He said that Little Ray would stay up for days without going to bed and then get sick and be in the bed for two or three days. Well, I knew he was sick a lot, but never made the connection. Little Ray would tell me that his daddy was mad at him because he was standing his ground sometimes and would not bow down and do what he said like he always has and that he was starting rumors about him to get him in trouble. He said his dad was the one taking drugs with alcohol and that he was the problem. I really didn't know who to believe, but in my heart I knew they were both telling the truth. They were regularly getting into fights and arguments. I prayed every day that one of them would not hurt or kill the other in anger. I hated getting a phone call from either one of them because I knew it would not be good. I have been on the phone with one of them and they would be so mad at the other that they were threatening to kill them. I knew they both carried loaded guns with them everywhere. I would get off the phone with them and hit my knees and start interceding for them that God would calm the situation without anyone getting hurt. God always stepped in and no one would get seriously hurt.

I remember back when Ray and I were still together, the two pivot irrigation systems collided with each other and Little Ray was supposed to be watching it. When Ray got the call, I could tell in a matter of seconds that some kind of disaster had happened. He was so mad and cursing Little Ray until his face was turning red and the veins on his neck were popping out. He threw the phone so hard that it knocked a hole in our bedroom wall and tore the phone to pieces. He stormed out of the house headed for the farm in a rage ready to hurt Little Ray for what happened. I started praying immediately that he would not hurt him. I kept praying until I got a phone call from Little Ray telling me he was ok. He said his dad threw a hammer at him and when it missed him he started chasing him with it. Luckily he didn't get hurt. I ask you-does it pay to pray? Does God hear our prayers? You bet it does. God is a God of miracles. I and my children are living proof of that.

CHAPTER 21

My Daughter Is Leaving Me?

Kalli and I were always close when she was little. I took her to church from the moment she was born. She was dedicated to God when she was only a couple months old. I always dressed her cute in her little dresses and hair bows. She was always the center of attention wherever she went because of her beautiful long hair. It was down below her knees. When she turned 13 years old, she started staying with her dad a lot. I found out once after she had stayed with him for the weekend that he decided to go to our camp on Toledo Bend which was about 50 miles from home. It was well after midnight so he was very drunk and drugged up. When they got about half way there, he was so messed up that he pulled over and had her drive the rest of the way. Needless to say, he passed out and she was left alone to drive about 20 miles in the dark on unfamiliar roads at 13 years of age. She said she was very scared but that she was more scared of the way her dad was driving. It scared me to death to think of what could have happened.

I knew something was up because he was asking her to stay over more often and he never did that before. She used to cry herself to sleep at night in the bed up next to me because her dad would not even answer her phone calls or call her back for days and sometimes weeks. We were not divorced yet because I dropped the case after all his threats. She stayed a couple times for several weeks at a time without coming home. Once it was time for her to come home and I could tell she acted funny over the phone. I went out to the farm to pick her up at Little Ray's house. No one was home except her. She walked out on the porch to come to the car. When I saw her my heart fell down in my stomach and I thought I was going to be sick. All her long hair that was all the way down past her knees was cut off and now it barely touched her shoulders. She had on a pair of jeans and a T-shirt. She had never owned a pair of jeans before. Her ears had been pierced and she had earrings in her ears. I had raised her in the Pentecostal church and this was totally against what she had been taught. My heart actually hurt as I watched her walk to the car. She was crying because she did not want to face me. Everybody else had left her there to face me alone. She got in the car still crying and we left headed for home. There was complete silence for a long time as I didn't know what to say and neither did she. I didn't want to get too upset and say the wrong thing and push her more toward her dad. I did not want to lose her to his deceitfulness. He thought this was all funny and tried to blame it on somebody else.

She continued to go to her dad's house quite often. Her dad and I had been separated for over 2 years now and I wanted to go ahead and get a divorce and put all this in the past and start over a new life. I had been praying about it for months but was still too afraid to do anything for fear of his threats. In January 2005 I was praying desperately for an answer. I had to know that God was with me. This is what I wrote in my journal:

January 13, 2005

It's been 2 years and 3 months since Ray and I separated. I want to go thru with the divorce but have been afraid. I've been praying about what to do and I've fasted too. Tuesday morning I prayed that if this is God's will for me then give me a word about it that I would not be afraid and know that God is in this. I opened my Bible and read in II Chronicles 16: 7-9. Verse 8 (revised) "Weren't' you faced with a great many chariots and horsemen and yet because you relied on God he delivered you? God looks all over the world to show himself strong for those with a perfect heart." In other words, "You needed me before and since you relied on me because no one else could help, I kept you safe and worked everything out."

Then He took me to II Chronicles 20: 15. "Thus saith the Lord unto you. Be not afraid nor dismayed by reason of this great multitude. For the battle is not yours, but God's." God is so good to show me a second time that He is with me. He will fight this battle for me. He will keep me safe. He will work out everything.

How could I go wrong with God on my side? Still, I wanted to know I was doing the right thing, that if this was God's leading and not mine, so I prayed that if He wanted me to do this that I would get an appointment with my lawyer one day this week on my 1:00 o'clock lunch hour. So I called as soon s I got to work and told her I needed to come during lunch one day this week and she said, "How about today! 1:00 o'clock."

OK God. I'm going thru with this. You have spoken 3 times today so why should I be afraid? The papers should be ready to be signed today and Ray will get them next week. I have a real peace about doing this even though fear tries to grip me sometimes when I think of his reaction to this. God has been with me through so much and has never let me down. I trust Him to work everything out."

She said she had an appointment available on my lunch break and could I come today. Today? Oh my God! I said yes before I could back out. I hung up the phone with a lump in my throat and trembling hands knowing I had an answer from God and now I had to act on it. I hurried over on my lunch break to the lawyer's office and pulled around back so my car couldn't be seen. I was so afraid that Ray would see me or find out that I was seeing a lawyer. He would be so mad. I had him served with the papers this time and he started calling me asking me not to do this and to just go through his lawyer and get the divorce. I stood my ground and kept my lawyer. He received the papers and agreed to everything except that it would be in Kalli's best interest for her to live with him instead of me. I already granted him joint custody but she should live with me. I'm her mother. I always took care of her and saw about her even when her dad wasn't around. How could he even ask for her to live with him and have anybody think it would be in her best interest. Kalli was still staying with him then so I called her since she was of the age to decide herself and asked what she wanted to do. She told me she wanted to live with her dad. My heart was broke. Of course, why would she want to live with me? I make her go to church and school and have nothing fun to do at the house. He lets her miss school. She doesn't have to go to church. She can ride four-wheelers and jet skis and have pool parties. Duh, what was I thinking? I told her that I understood and it was her choice but I wanted her to know that He would not have to pay me child support for her if she agreed to live with him even if she later decided to come back home. She said she was ok with that and she wanted to stay. I knew what he was doing but I wasn't going to tell Kalli because I didn't want to cause any more hurt concerning her dad.

So, I signed off on the agreement even though I knew it wasn't right. The next weekend after we signed the papers, Ray had his secretary bring Kalli home and drop her off. She came in crying and apologizing. She realized what had happened after it was done. She said her dad hadn't even been home in several days and he sent word to take her home. It was almost a year before he invited her back. So, he got away with not paying any child support because he made the courts believe that Kalli was going to live with him.

After a couple months, our court date came up to finalize our divorce. I was so nervous and afraid of what he might do when we got to court. I left work and headed for the court house. When I arrived, his lawyer told me that Ray didn't want to come and had signed the necessary papers that made his lawyer to be able to speak for him. We all went up before the judge and she granted the divorce. A lump started coming in my throat to think of what this really means. Ray and I are no longer married. After 26 years of good times and bad times we were no longer husband and wife. I knew I was doing the right thing and that it had to be done, but it hurt. I felt like I had been to a funeral. I couldn't even talk to my lawyer or his when she dismissed us because the tears started flowing harder and harder. I just started walking to my car and did not look back. I was supposed to go back to work, but I went home and sobbed the rest of the day.

Ladies conference was the next week and God really changed me during my stay. I rented a motel room so I could be alone with God. I went determined to come back different, and that I did. I did not visit with the other ladies or go out to eat at fancy restaurants or go shopping like I usually do. I went to every service and when there wasn't a service going on, I was back in my motel room on the floor crying out to God. I took the bedspread off the spare bed and put it on the floor and I fell on my knees in desperation for God to help me. I wanted to be free. I wanted to be whole. I wanted the joy of the Holy Ghost to take over my life and rid me of the depression and oppression and fear and anger that I had lived with for so many years. I wanted to be able to share with other ladies what God had done for me and how he brought me safely out of a dangerous situation that could have ended in tragedy. I could have been the one on the 6 o'clock news. I wanted to be able to encourage other ladies to trust God to guide them in every decision they make because he sees ahead and he knows what is best to carry out the plan he has for your life. I wanted to be able to tell them that God doesn't give up on you because the plans he had for you went sour, especially when there was nothing you could do. He always has another plan for your life when you fully trust him and obey his ways. I wanted to tell them that God loves them personally and cares about every little detail of their life. I never really grasped that until I went through all of this.

I prayed for hours over the next few days. As I lay on the floor in that motel, so desperate before God, he came down into that room and saturated my whole body, mind and soul with a peace beyond compare and a joy that flowed like a river. I was saturated in His love. I could no longer speak words but utterances of the Holy Ghost. I was in the presence of the Almighty God. His Spirit and my spirit were one. I cannot completely describe to you what happened that day in that motel room. It was beyond compare to anything I had ever experienced before. This was the beginning of my new walk with God.

CHAPTER 22

Father Against Son?

Things kept getting worse between Big Ray and Little Ray. Little Ray was busted for drugs a couple times. Every time he did something his dad didn't like, he would make him move out of his trailer out on the farm and take his truck away from him. The truck and trailer both belonged to Big Ray so he had the upper hand. After a few days, he would call

Little Ray and ask him to come back because he needed him on the farm. I wrote in my journal as follows (in part):

June 28, 2005

Ray called tonight to tell me how bad a shape Little Ray was in taking drugs. Little Ray said it was his dad in bad shape. They were furious at each other over something and while I was on the phone with Little Ray, Big Ray drives up to his house. I knew that meant trouble. He said he would call me back. He hung up the phone in an angry rage. I shake to think of what could have happened. I don't know who is telling the truth, though I think and know in my heart- they both are. Both of them have a serious problem that will cost them their life one day. Alcohol and drugs are destroying them- their bodies and their families. I got down on the floor and cried out to God with all my heart that He would spare us from tragedy and not let them end up in hell tonight. I pray that some-how and some way they would want help and get help before all our lives are ruined. After praying, I was just waiting on God. I was sitting there numb; my face swollen from crying so hard and God said, "My grace is sufficient! My grace is sufficient! Over and over I heard that in my mind. What does that mean? Grace for what? What is going to happen? I got the dictionary and grace means "favor shown in granting a delay". Thank you Jesus for delaying tragedy one more time in my family. Please save them!!!"

Kalli was staying more with her dad now so I had a lot of time to myself when I wasn't working. He didn't have any rules at his house so naturally she liked to stay there. He even let her quit school. He let her have friends over for parties and he would cook for them and let them drink beer. She finally went and got her GED and then went to work for him at his other business.

I love both of my kids more than I could ever tell you and it hurt me so much to see them deceived and tortured by their dad. He had such a hold on them just like he did me at one time. They were almost like puppets in his hands and when they did not cooperate, he took vengeance out on them that was way worse than the crime. Sometimes I would ask God why he allowed him to keep torturing my family and have them so afraid and paranoid all the time. Sometimes I would spend my whole lunch hour on the floor praying for God to do something to change this situation. I would get up and wash my face and go back to work knowing that God is watching and He will handle it in His own time and in His own way.

With all this time alone, my prayer life got stronger and stronger. I would come home from work and eat dinner and then read a book or watch a preaching video or a Christian movie or listen to a cd. I didn't want to watch TV. I hardly ever watched TV during the week. I would sometimes watch a Hallmark movie on the weekends. I wanted to learn more about the ways of God. I wanted to be in His presence, surrounded by good, clean thoughts and sounds that were so different than what I used to live in. I wanted nothing but a pure, godly atmosphere in my home because I wanted and needed God to live there with me. I wanted every part of my life to be pleasing to God. Don't get me wrong. I'm not condemning anyone that watches TV or any other thing that may occupy your time. I still enjoy these things myself. I was just given the opportunity to have time alone with God on a daily basis with no other obligations to anyone. I felt a call on my life to become closer to God and have a relationship with him to where He could talk to me and use me in prayer and intercession. I loved this time alone with God. He gave me scriptures such as Leviticus 20:26 which says, "And ye shall be holy unto me; for I the Lord am holy, and have severed you from other people, that ye should be mine." And also Numbers 16:9 which says, "Seemeth it but a small thing unto you, that the God of Israel hath separated you from the congregation of Israel, to bring you near to himself to do the service of the tabernacle of the Lord, and to stand before the congregation to minister unto them?"

In my praying and studying the Word of God is where I really learned to communicate with God. I prayed with a sincere heart, not with beautiful words that people would like to hear. I did not rush. I would lay prostrate on the floor sometimes in deep, consecrated prayer to God and when I could not pray any more, I would just lay there and God would talk to me. Not in a voice I could hear out loud, but one I could hear in my heart. I learned to meditate on God and shut out the whole world around me. I felt it such a privilege to be in the presence of God and to be called of God for a greater service. I knew I was not worthy to be called for anything, but God reminded me that it is not my worthiness, but His.

I eventually felt lead to teach a series to my ladies group on becoming a woman of excellence and becoming a woman of prayer. I come across some books that seemed to be perfect just by accident. The lesson was for me more than anyone else, but I prayed every week that at least one person would receive encouragement and really want to work on becoming excellent in everything she does and becoming a woman of prayer. I wanted to help some lady to feel better about herself because God loves her and I did to. I pray that at least one lady in that group was helped in some way that made a positive difference in her life.

CHAPTER 23

Our Agreement

On August of 2005, Ray and I made a community property settlement agreement. I was to receive my house and car and a few other things. I also was to receive monthly alimony until death or I remarry. Everything was supposed to be lien free, but through a mess up in wording of the documents, he got by with just paying the note on the house. He was to get everything else including our home and our lake house, both businesses, and all bank accounts, CDs and vehicles. I gladly settled for that if he would just leave me alone and not threaten and terrorize me anymore. I was so afraid of him. He would still drive by my house very slowly and park down the street and just sit there. Sometimes he would be sitting in the parking lot when I got out of church or when I came out of the grocery store. The drugs and alcohol was getting worse and sometimes he wouldn't even remember his outbursts of anger. Every month I had to call numerous times for him to give me my alimony money. I asked him to pay my house off a couple times, trying to show him how much he would be saving by doing so. I was so afraid that something would happen that he would default in some way and I would lose my home. Eventually, in 2008, he told me that he had a CD coming up for renewal in a couple months and he would think about paying off my house. When the time came, I called to see if he would pay it off and he said that he wasn't worried about paying off my house. He had only been paying the minimum on it each month. After all, both of his houses were paid for. It was just another way to keep me under his control. I told him then that I wouldn't ask him any more…and I didn't. I found out that you can go back to court within 3 years of your settlement and re-sue for more than you settled for in a community property settlement if you received less than half and have a good reason. Well that fit me. I had only received less than 5% because I was too afraid to ask for more. I really didn't want him to have to sell anything, I just wanted what was mine to be out of his control and since he was being so ridiculous about paying for my little dab of stuff I got, I decided I would ask for more.

CHAPTER 24

The 2 ½ Year Nightmare

I had just met a wonderful man, Don, a few months prior to this whom I married on April 26, 2008. We had known each other for a long time and were neighbors but I hadn't seen him in several years. His wife had died of cancer. He came to my office one day for an insurance quote and we've been together ever since. I never dreamed of having a husband that would be so good to me. It was after we were married that I finally got the papers filed to start the beginning of a 2 ½ year nightmare.

The Nightmare Begins

I look back now and see just how much God had His hand in this whole situation. I filed the necessary papers to sue him to at least pay off my house and give me a little money too. Since he was being so negligent about paying, I thought I should ask for more. The papers were filed 1 week before the 3 year deadline of which I would have received nothing more. Lawyers were asking to see financials and other paperwork and just like I thought, Ray started trying to call me. I didn't want to talk to him because I knew he would just threaten me and keep me afraid to go anywhere by myself. Don never would give him my phone number so I never talked to him on the phone. I was watchful when I went somewhere because I did not want to run in to him. Sometimes he would drive into the parking lot of our church and try to get one of the men to come in and get me. He called there too and got a little ugly a couple times because they would not go get me. I just thought when we divorced and I remarried that I would be free of him.

He wanted to get ugly in our paperwork and say things that were mostly lies just for embarrassment. Everything in his life was turmoil and he wanted everybody else to be miserable too. He no longer had anyone living with him. He and Little Ray were still at odds as well.

In February 2009 on a Monday morning, Kalli called to tell me Little Ray's mobile home had burned down during the night. No one was home, thank God.

Immediately, I knew in my heart that Big Ray had something to do with it. I couldn't prove it, but I knew it. He had threatened that to me several times. I got on the floor and cried out to God, "How much longer are you going to let Ray torture me and my kids? Please don't let him get away with this. He has hurt too many people and gotten by with it. He has beaten up and almost killed people thru the years and always gets away free. Please stop him from hurting us. We can't take any more."

No one knows what happened about the fire. He eventually got the insurance check for it and pocketed it without giving Little Ray and his family any of it to start over even though he had them fill out insurance papers on what they had inside. They lost everything and Big Ray got the money.

CHAPTER 25

A Horrible Sight

I had to go to a deposition with Big Ray and our lawyers a couple weeks after that and when he walked in I could hardly believe my eyes. My heart jumped into my throat as I saw what horrible shape he was in. I had not seen him up close for several months. His skin was a purplish-red color, almost blue, very swollen all over- almost unrecognizable. I didn't dare ask what was wrong with him but I knew it must be horrible. He hugged me real hard when I walked in and he shook hands with my lawyer. We had our meeting and everybody went home without incident. That was the last time I saw him.

Don and I left to go to Australia for the month of March 2009. What a wonderful trip! We got back home on March 26. I called Kalli to tell her we were home and asked about her dad. She started crying and said she was worried about him because he looked so bad and could not stay awake. She called me 2 days later and said he had been found dead in his bed. 49 years old. The report said "of natural causes", but there is nothing natural about dying at age 49. My heart hurt to know he died never getting his life straightened out. I can only pray that he got to talk to God before he went out. Later it was determined that he had liver failure from too much alcohol.

I had to go over to his house to let the kids in because I still had a key. A nervous feeling always came over me when I went in his house, but it wasn't so bad that day. Little Ray found things on the counter that were lying on the bar at his house the night it burned which confirmed what I already knew. That made me feel sick to my stomach.

I went to the funeral to bring closure. I knew I had to see him to close that part of my life. As I stood there thinking maybe he could somehow feel how sorry I was for him that his life ended like that, I couldn't help but feel relieved to know that I didn't have to be afraid of him any more… and neither would my kids. I know how that must sound, but don't judge me until you've been in my shoes. I still had nightmares pretty often, for about another year after that, and that was bad enough.

Now that Big Ray was gone, what do we do now? Our suit was put on hold for 6 months while the necessary paperwork was done to get it going again. The difference is- now I'm suing my kids. Oh God. How did it turn into this? I just wanted a good home and some income to supplement my job. I just wanted to get back some of what I worked for all my life.

After 1 year and 7 months and a lot of stress and tears, we finally reached an agreement we could all be happy with. God restored to me what I lost and then some. I got back more than I ever expected. I was even awarded the .357 Magnum that I talked about in Chapter 9 and the .32 pistol he used in Chapter 14. I wanted them as trophies to show the devil and as a reminder that I serve a miracle-working God.

God blessed my kids to receive a good part as well.

CHAPTER 26

A Happy Ending

God has been so good to me and my family. I live in a peaceful home now with more love and kindness than I ever imagined and the best husband in the world. I have been blessed to work on the turf farm as owner/manager and have an income to live on and to bless God with. I still, as always, pay my tithes and offerings on what I bring home. I pay it first, before anything else comes out. I know that is why God has blessed me so. Thru everything, I always had enough money to buy groceries and pay my bills. Not because I gave a lot, but because I gave of what I had.

God took care of me through a lot of pain and hurt. Even when I doubted and feared, He was right there all along. He kept me safe when it should have been tragic because I called on His name when there was no other to call on. Now that's all behind me and I don't live in fear and dread anymore. I have a husband that I look forward to seeing every evening and we spend every spare minute we can together. We meet for lunch several times a week. Has God put His blessings on my life? Yes! Is God faithful? Yes. Is this really my life??? Yes! Yes! Thank you Jesus!

THE END

Made in the USA
Charleston, SC
11 February 2016